ABSOLUTE BEGINNERS
Voice

First Vocal Exercises

This helpful pull-out chart has taken a selection of the vocal exercises on pages 18–20 and organized them into a five-week beginner course. Once you have worked your way through this sheet, you will be able to tackle some of the more difficult exercises in the book and even create your own warm-up regimens.

As you begin your first vocal exercises, remember that it is vital to maintain a proper posture throughout. It is important to take these exercises only as high or low as is comfortable on any given day and never sing for more than twenty minutes without a break.

If your throat feels tight and constricted in the lower range while you are singing any of these exercises, it may help to think of "speaking" the pitches, sustaining the vowel as long as the rhythmic value of the note. If you are experiencing tension while singing in the upper range, sing through the passages on each of the five vowels to determine if one is more comfortable than the others. Then, modifying the exercise toward your favorite vowel, see if you can match the internal sensation to that vowel.

A few words about *glottal attack:* This is a type of attack that is produced when the vocal folds strike each other with a sort of "click" when attacking a vowel sound. It is best avoided at all costs as a beginner. Glottal attack can cause vocal tightness, fatigue, and other complications if overused. Pop singer Regina Spektor effectively uses glottal attack in some of her improvisational singing, but it should be used sparingly and only while you are under the guidance of a vocal teaching professional.

Note that in each exercise, I have listed various vowel and consonant/vowel combinations as options during vocalization. Each has its own benefits and potential challenges depending on the individual. As you become more confident, try mixing and matching the vowel sounds over all the exercises.

Vocal Exercises

We have included a male and female demonstration of every exercise. All exercises move in half steps—some move downward first, then upward; others move upward only. The best way to approach these exercises is to *listen* carefully to the demonstration before attempting it yourself. Listen to the vowel sounds and vocal tone, and notice how our vocalists only take a breath at the end of the phrase, while the pianist plays the next chord.

In the track following the demonstrations, you will have a chance to sing on your own to the piano backing. The pianist will play the notes of the exercise first, and then you start. This procedure will be repeated for each subsequent vowel. Please go only as high or low as is comfortable—it takes practice to extend your range so take it one small step at a time to avoid damaging your voice.

IPA Symbols

[u]	as in "b**oo**t"
[o]	as in "alth**ou**gh"
[ɔ]	as in "c**ou**gh"
[ɑ]	as in "f**a**ther"
[ə]	as in "g**u**t"
[ɛ]	as in "b**e**d"
[e]	as in "M**ay**"
[i]	as in "s**ee**"
[ð]	*th* as in "**th**e"
[ŋ]	*ng* as in "si**ng**"

Pull-Out Chart

Week 1

Start on **Track 1** if you are female and **Track 2** if you are male, and listen to our vocalist sing the five vowels, one after the other. Listen to the pitch carefully and try to match it before attempting yourself in **Track 3**.

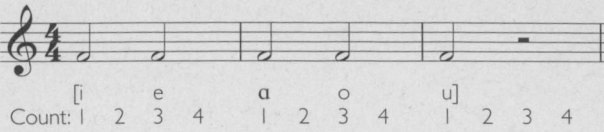

Warm-Up Exercises

Basic warm-ups are a great way to start off your practice sessions. In each exercise, keep phonation very smooth (*legato*), avoiding the sound of an "h" as you move through the notes of each exercise.

Try this series of five notes in a scale, ascending and descending:

Female
Track 4
Male
Track 5
Backing
Track 6

In this next exercise, we've added some syllables that help foster relaxation of the jaw. You should feel very supple as the jaw drops repeatedly. The jaw should be allowed to move freely during this exercise, but not unnaturally. Make sure you are getting a good breath before the phrase and keep the energy behind the breath moving through the phrase to the end. It may help to imagine singing a *crescendo* toward the end of each phrase.

Female
Track 10
Male
Track 11
Backing
Track 12

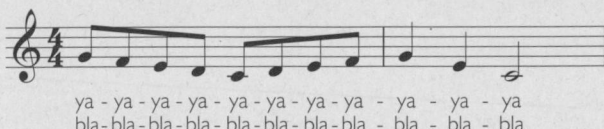

Tip

You might find that as you move upward in range, it is helpful to drop the jaw, increasing the mouth opening, to sing the top notes. Be aware of what you are doing physically when singing lower and higher. For example, do not move your head toward your chest as you go lower as that will impede the breath trying to come out of your throat and cause tension. Likewise, do not do raise your head when you sing high! Keep your head in the position as outlined in the Posture and Alignment chapter. Keep your throat open and relaxed, and be aware of tension anywhere in the body. If you feel tense, revisit the stretching and relaxation exercises on page 8.

Agility Exercise

Agility exercises will improve your movement between the upper and lower registers. If the voice feels strained and/or is going out of tune as the voice heads upward in the range, this can be a sign of singing too heavily in the lower voice and not allowing the voice to "flip" into the upper range. Drop your jaw and relax your throat. This will allow the voice to move freely into the upper range without having to strain.

Remember, only take this as high or low as is comfortable!

Female
Track 25
Male
Track 26
Backing
Track 27

Resonance Exercises

Really try to feel the "buzz" of resonance in your nasal cavity when you sing through these exercises. If you have trouble with the rolled "r" sound on "re-no-ne," try speaking these words in the following manner:

- Pdessure (pressure)
- Pday (pray)
- Kdaft (craft)

Use the syllables "kda kda kda kda" on any of the vocal exercises in this book. With practice, you may be able to reach a fully rolled "r" sound.

Female
Track 40
Male
Track 41
Backing
Track 42

Female
Track 43
Male
Track 44
Backing
Track 45

Week 2

Warm-Up Exercises

Female	Male	Backing
Track 4	Track 5	Track 6

Female	Male	Backing
Track 7	Track 8	Track 9

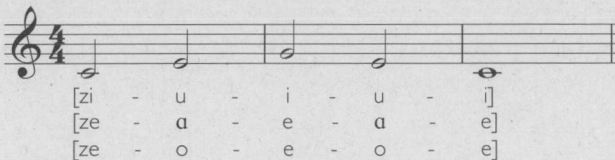

[zi – u – i – u – i]
[ze – ɑ – e – ɑ – e]
[ze – o – e – o – e]

Female	Male	Backing
Track 10	Track 11	Track 12

Agility Exercises

Notice the little slurs (⌣) and accent marks (>) in the exercise below. This means that you sing each group of two notes smoothly, with slightly more emphasis on the first (not too much, however). Listen to our vocalists demonstrate and you'll hear the result you should be aiming for.

Female	Male	Backing
Track 16	Track 17	Track 18

[zi _____ e _____]

Female	Male	Backing
Track 25	Track 26	Track 27

Resonance Exercises

When you hum ("m"), keep your teeth slightly apart behind closed lips, and jaw very relaxed.

Female	Male	Backing
Track 37	Track 38	Track 39

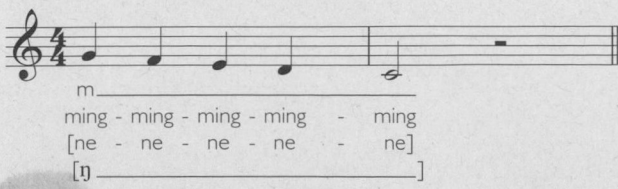

m _____
ming - ming - ming - ming - ming
[ne - ne - ne - ne - ne]
[ŋ _____]

Female	Male	Backing
Track 43	Track 44	Track 45

Week 3

Warm-Up Exercises

Female	Male	Backing
Track 4	Track 5	Track 6

Female	Male	Backing
Track 7	Track 8	Track 9

Female	Male	Backing
Track 10	Track 11	Track 12

Agility Exercises

Female	Male	Backing
Track 16	Track 17	Track 18

Female	Male	Backing
Track 19	Track 20	Track 21

[zi _____ u _____]
[ze _____ o _____]
[ze _____ ɑ _____]

Female	Male	Backing
Track 25	Track 26	Track 27

Resonance Exercises

Female	Male	Backing
Track 37	Track 38	Track 39

Female	Male	Backing
Track 40	Track 41	Track 42

Female	Male	Backing
Track 46	Track 47	Track 48

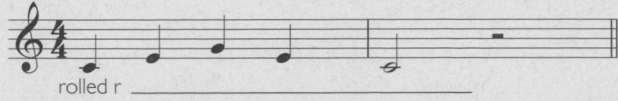

rolled r _____

WEEK 4

Warm-Up Exercises

Female	Male	Backing
Track 4	Track 5	Track 6

Female	Male	Backing
Track 10	Track 11	Track 12

Now let's try some real words! The exercise below is great for practicing your enunciation. Remember to sing through the vowels and use the consonants to propel the phrase. Refer back to page 17 and remind yourself of the correct way to enunciate words while singing.

Female	Male	Backing
Track 13	Track 14	Track 15

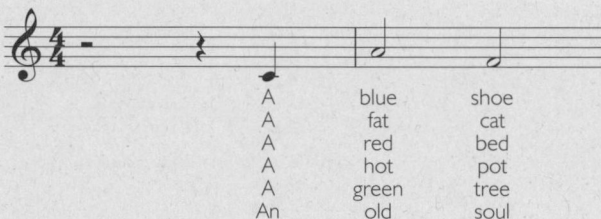

Agility Exercises

Female	Male	Backing
Track 19	Track 20	Track 21

Female	Male	Backing
Track 22	Track 23	Track 24

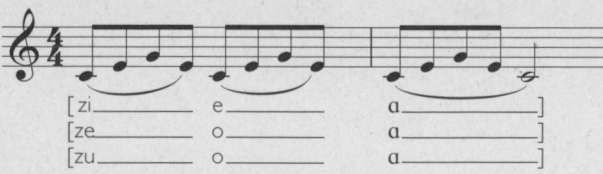

Female	Male	Backing
Track 25	Track 26	Track 27

Resonance Exercises

Female	Male	Backing
Track 37	Track 38	Track 39

Female	Male	Backing
Track 43	Track 44	Track 45

Female	Male	Backing
Track 46	Track 47	Track 48

WEEK 5

Warm-Up Exercises

Female	Male	Backing
Track 43	Track 44	Track 45

Female	Male	Backing
Track 10	Track 11	Track 12

Female	Male	Backing
Track 13	Track 14	Track 15

Agility Exercises

Female	Male	Backing
Track 22	Track 23	Track 24

Female	Male	Backing
Track 25	Track 26	Track 27

Female	Male	Backing
Track 28	Track 29	Track 30

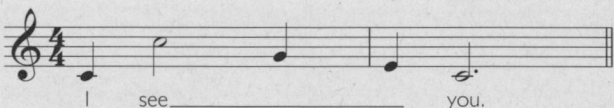

Female	Male	Backing
Track 31	Track 32	Track 33

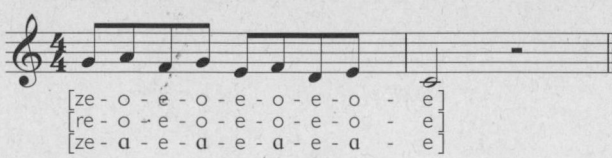

Resonance Exercises

Female	Male	Backing
Track 37	Track 38	Track 39

Female	Male	Backing
Track 40	Track 41	Track 42

Female	Male	Backing
Track 46	Track 47	Track 48